World-Changing SCIENTISTS

Leonardo da Vinci

Alix Wood

PowerKiDS press

New York

Published in 2019 by Rosen Publishing
29 East 21st Street, New York, NY 10010

Cataloging-in-Publication Data

Names: Wood, Alix.
Title: Leonardo da Vinci / Alix Wood.
Description: New York : PowerKids Press, 2019. | Series: World-changing scientists
| Includes glossary and index.
Identifiers: LCCN ISBN 9781538337783 (pbk.) | ISBN 9781538337776 (library
bound) | ISBN 9781538337790 (6 pack)
Subjects: LCSH: Leonardo, da Vinci, 1452-1519--Juvenile literature.| Artists--Italy--
Biography--Juvenile literature.| Scientists--Italy--Biography--Juvenile literature.
Classification: LCC N6923.L33 W64 2019 | DDC 709.2 B--dc23

Adaptations to North American edition © 2019
by Rosen Publishing

Produced for Rosen Publishing by Alix Wood Books
Designed by Alix Wood
Editor: Eloise Macgregor

Photo credits:
Cover, 1, 5, 8, 9 bottom, 19, 22 © Adobe Stock Images; 6 © Josep Torta; 7 © agmcat;
9 top, 16, 20, 23 bottom © Shutterstock; 12 © Michael Reed; 15 © Léonard de Serres, Château
du Clos Lucé; 21, 26 bottom, 27 © Alix Wood; 24 © Museum of Fine Arts, Budapest; all other
images are in the public domain

Printed in the United States of America

CPSIA compliance information: Batch #CS18PK: For further information contact Rosen Publishing, New
York, New York at 1-800-542-2595.

Contents

World -Changing Scientist
Leonardo da Vinci

Leonardo da Vinci was born in Italy in 1452. He is probably best known for his painting, the *Mona Lisa*. He was not just an artist, however. Leonardo was an engineer, mathematician, **architect**, and scientist. Da Vinci is thought to be one of the most talented people to have ever lived!

A portrait of Leonardo da Vinci by Francesco Melzi, one of his pupils.

The *Mona Lisa* by Leonardo da Vinci is probably the most famous painting in the world.

Science Notes

Leonardo da Vinci's interest in science helped him become such a great artist. He was fascinated by **anatomy**. He studied people and animals to try to understand how their bones and muscles worked. He would examine the corpses of both humans and animals and make detailed drawings of them. This work meant that he understood what lay beneath the skin, and he could draw the muscles on a body so they looked amazingly lifelike.

Leonardo lived during a period known as the **Renaissance**. It was a time of new ideas in art, literature, science, religion, math, and **politics**. The printing press was developed at this time, which meant that new ideas could be spread easily in books. Renaissance means "rebirth." Someone skilled in many areas, like Leonardo was, is sometimes known as a **Renaissance man**.

Europe

The Renaissance started in Italy.

A Childhood in Italy

L eonardo was born in 1452 in the small village of Anchiano, in the Italian countryside. His house was surrounded by vineyards and olive groves. Leonardo's parents, Ser Piero and Caterina, were not married. This was probably because Caterina was from a lower **social class**. She went on to marry someone else, and had five more children.

Leonardo lived with his father. His father married three times, and had thirteen more children. Leonardo seemed to have a good relationship with his stepmothers. He once wrote a greeting to his father's last wife, calling her "my dear beloved mother."

The house in Anchiano, where Leonardo is believed to have been born.

6

Incredibly, we know the exact time and date of Leonardo's birth, as his grandfather wrote it in a notebook that was discovered in 1939.

"1452: There was born to me a grandson, the child of Ser Piero my son on 15 April, a Saturday, at the third hour of the night. He was named Lionardo."

In those days, the "hours of the night" started at sunset, so we know Leonardo was born at 10:00 p.m., three hours after a 7:00 p.m. sunset. It was quite common then to spell names in a number of different ways, so to spell Leonardo "Lionardo" would not be unusual.

The view from Leonardo's house.

In Leonardo's time, having unmarried parents could restrict the things you were allowed to do. Leonardo could not attend university, or be a doctor or a lawyer. His stepmother, grandparents, and his Uncle Francesco helped give him a good basic education.

Leonardo's interest in science was encouraged by his uncle. Uncle Francesco was just 16 years older than Leonardo. They spent a lot of time together wandering the countryside looking at nature. Leonardo's grandfather showed him how to keep a journal. This habit helped him record his discoveries and ideas. His journals were full of many different things, from shopping lists to diagrams showing how to build a tank!

Science Notes

Keeping a notebook is an important way to record scientific discoveries. Scientists usually keep a lab notebook to jot down their ideas and keep track of the materials and steps needed for their experiments. Scientists can record results in their notebook, and use their notes to help remember all the details when they write up their report.

Lab Notebook

Leonardo's designs for an armored tank, taken from one of his journals.

Even at an early age, Leonardo did not like to stick to one subject. He was said to have a good knowledge of books, he played the **lyre** beautifully, and was so good at math that he often outsmarted his teachers. He was also very good at art. It is said that when Leonardo was 14 years old, he painted a dragon that looked so lifelike it scared his father!

a lyre

There were some gaps in Leonardo's education. He never learned **Latin**, a language most well-educated Renaissance men would have known. He also never learned to write using his right hand. Left-handed children at that time were usually forced to write using their right hand, *because people believed that the devil was left-handed*.

Artist and Sculptor

Leonardo's father realized his son had a great artistic talent. He took his son's sketches to Andrea del Verrocchio, a painter, sculptor, and goldsmith who ran an important workshop in Florence. Verrocchio immediately recognized Leonardo's skill, and persuaded Leonardo's father to let his son train with him. As a result, when Leonardo was around 15 years old, he moved to Florence to become an artist's **apprentice**.

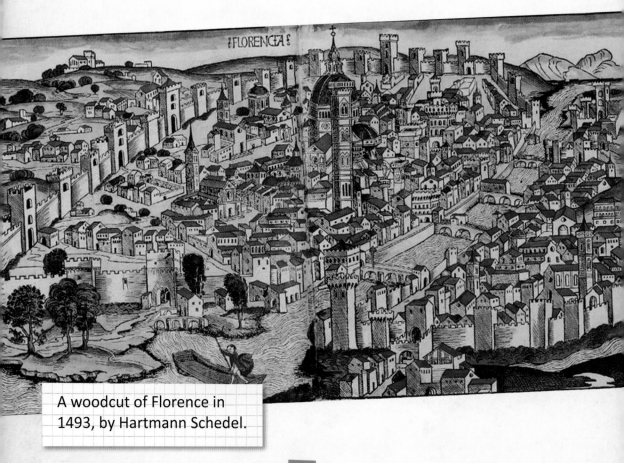

A woodcut of Florence in 1493, by Hartmann Schedel.

Science Notes

The Italian city of Florence was one of the main centers of the Renaissance. It was a time of exploration and discovery. Explorers were sailing into unknown seas. They reached new land, and trade routes were established. This new knowledge of what our planet looked like would be essential for the scientists of the future. Mapmakers based in Florence helped explorers plan and record their journeys. Bankers from the city helped pay for their explorations.

An early Italian map of the world.

Many great artists lived and worked in Florence. Why should art and science be connected? Renaissance art and architecture used math. Artists and scholars believed works of art were best when created using mathematical laws and reasoning.

After Leonardo had finished his apprenticeship, he left Verrochio's studio and began work as an artist. He got a reputation for not finishing his work on time. A church in Milan asked him to do a painting for them, and gave him seven months to complete it. He finally delivered the painting 25 years later! Leonardo wanted a new challenge. He wrote to the ruler of Milan, Duke Ludovico Sforza, and offered his services as a military inventor and engineer. The first job he was given was to create a giant sculpture.

Leonardo's Great Horse

First, Leonardo made a clay model of the giant horse. It stood 24 feet (7.3 m) tall. The bronze version was never made. Sforza decided the metal needed to make the statue should be used for weapons instead. Leonardo's engineering skills impressed Sforza, though, and he hired him to invent and design new weapons.

This replica in Grand Rapids, Michigan, was built using Leonardo's drawings.

Art Meets Science

Creating a giant sculpture needs a good understanding of science and engineering. Leonardo originally wanted his horse to be rearing up on its back legs. But how could the statue be made to support the weight of the front half of the horse? Leonardo's solution was to have an enemy soldier cowering under the horse, whose raised arm could support the front legs.

Leonardo's sketch, showing the soldier.

Eventually, Leonardo decided to create a trotting horse instead. This was still not simple, as the statue was so large. He drew diagrams showing how he thought the **casting** should be done. To cast the statue in one piece, he devised a system of timed **furnaces** that opened in a sequence. The furnaces were controlled by sensors which, as the **molten** bronze reached them, sent out a signal to open the next furnace!

Making War Machines

Despite not completing his horse statue, Leonardo continued to work for the Duke of Sforza for 17 years. In his first letter introducing himself to the Duke, he had promised to design all kinds of weapons. He wrote:

"I can make armored cars, safe and unassailable, which will enter the closed ranks of the enemy with their artillery, and no company of soldiers is so great that it will not break through them. And behind these our infantry will be able to follow quite unharmed...""

Leonardo set to work inventing war machines. One of his most terrifying inventions was an armored tank. Many hundreds of years before tanks in warfare became commonplace, Leonardo drew the design below. The tank was to be pushed along using hand cranks. Eight men hid inside, working the cranks and firing the weapons. The tank was armed with 36 guns pointing in all directions.

Leonardo's drawing of a tank.

A model of Leonardo's tank, with a cutaway showing the wheels and cranks.

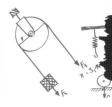

Science Notes

Leonardo's Tank Design

It appears that Leonardo's tank was never built, and it was not until World War I, almost 400 years later, that any army used a tank in warfare. Leonardo's design was superior to the World War I tanks in an ingenious way: it used a sloped armor plate. This angle increases the amount of protective material something hitting the tank would have to pass through without adding any more armor or increasing the weight of the tank. This sloped design also **deflects** the force of anything hitting the tank, which helps protect it. The World War I tank's largest surfaces had flat panels that were much more easily damaged by flying **ammunition**!

Keeping Secrets

Leonardo had a clever way of keeping notes. He wrote back to front using mirror writing. He used mirror writing on documents that he wanted no one but himself to read. Can you read this?

No one knows the true reason why Leonardo used mirror writing, but he may have been making it harder for people to read his notes and steal his ideas. He may also have wanted to hide his scientific ideas from the Roman Catholic Church, whose teachings sometimes disagreed with what Leonardo was discovering. The most likely answer is that Leonardo used mirror writing because he was left-handed. Writing from left to right smeared the wet ink as his hand moved across it.

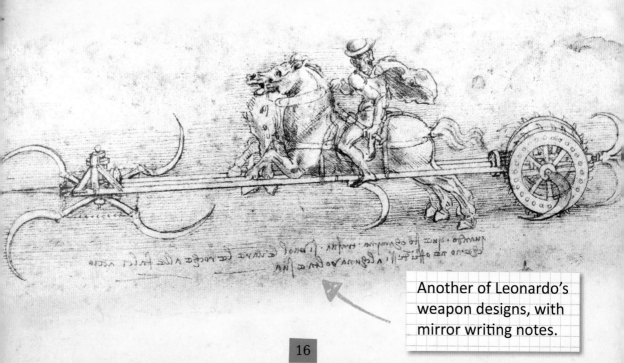

Another of Leonardo's weapon designs, with mirror writing notes.

How Do We Know Leonardo Was Left-handed?

Imagine shading an area using close-together **parallel** lines. If you're right-handed, you'll probably draw strokes from the top right of the sheet to the lower left. If you're left-handed, you'll probably sketch lines from top left to lower right. Many of Leonardo's drawings were shaded using lines that went from top left to lower right.

The shading on this portrait by Leonardo looks as if it was done using his left hand.

A Hand Injury?

Some people think that Leonardo may have become left-handed as the result of an injury to his right hand in early adulthood. It is said Leonardo could draw forward with one hand while writing backward with the other!

The Borgia's Military Engineer

Between 1502 and 1503, da Vinci worked in Florence as a military engineer for Cesare Borgia. Borgia was a powerful nobleman and military commander. Leonardo was asked to inspect and direct all Borgia's military construction. Leonardo also drew useful city plans and maps for his new employer.

Leonardo was one of the first mapmakers to draw maps from above, using a bird's-eye view. He was also the first mapmaker known to have used different colors to show different heights of mountain.

Cesare Borgia (left) found Leonardo's detailed maps (below) very useful when he planned attacks on his enemies.

Leonardo's map of the city of Imola.

Who Was Cesare Borgia?

Cesare Borgia was the son of Pope Alexander VI. His first career was in the church. He was made Bishop of Pamplona at age 15, and archbishop of Valencia at 17. By the age of 18, he was a cardinal. When Cesare's elder brother was murdered, his father made him head of his army at just 20 years old. He wanted to bring all the central Italian cities under Pope Alexander's control. Cesare was ruthless and power hungry. When his father died, the new pope disliked the Borgia family. Cesare was arrested and sent to a Spanish prison. He escaped, and was later killed in an ambush while helping attack a castle for his brother-in-law, King John of Navarre.

The detailed information on Leonardo's maps would have been very useful to Cesare Borgia. Knowing the landscape of a battlefield makes waging war much easier. Leonardo mapped all the rivers in the area, which would help Cesare's army plan their route, and make the most effective attack.

Leonardo helped **survey** a canal being built from Cesena to the Porto Cesenatico in Italy. To view the canal from the right angle for his bird's-eye view, Leonardo is said to have climbed to the top of a beautiful tower that once stood at Cesenatico.

Studying Anatomy

Anatomy is the science that studies the structure of humans and animals. The word "anatomy" comes from an ancient Greek word meaning "to dissect," or cut up. Studying anatomy usually means cutting up a body in order to study its internal parts.

Leonardo was fascinated by how bodies worked. He drew very detailed drawings of the human body. He felt that to draw a person or animal accurately, he needed to understand what lay beneath the skin.

Leonardo was given permission to dissect the dead bodies of criminals. He worked by candlelight, holding a cloth over his mouth and nose to lessen the smell of the rotting corpses.

"The human foot is a masterpiece of engineering and a work of art."

LEONARDO DA VINCI

How to Create Scientific Drawings

A scientific drawing is very different from a work of art. Leonardo excelled at both kinds of drawing. He created the first full anatomical drawings in a notebook he called *On the Human Figure*, which has been used by medical students for hundreds of years.

What makes a good scientific drawing? The important thing for scientists is that the illustration or diagram shows all the necessary parts clearly, accurately, and to scale, and contains the information the drawing is intended to show. To create a good scientific drawing, you should:

- Use a sharp pencil and unlined paper.
- Leave room around your image for your labels.
- Create clear outlines, do not sketch.
- Use dots to shade any darker areas.
- Only draw what you see, not what you think you should see.
- Label the parts using solid straight lines that touch the structure.
- Do not cross label lines.

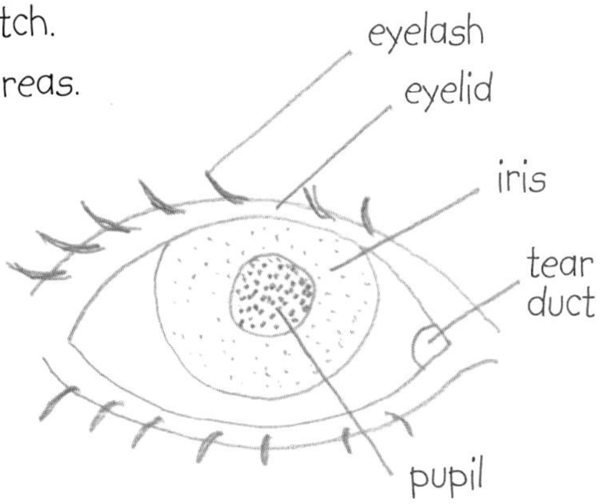

eyelash
eyelid
iris
tear duct
pupil

Try drawing a scientific diagram yourself.

Amazing Inventions

Throughout his life, Leonardo thought up inventions. He designed all kinds of things, from weapons and flying machines to robots and tools. Leonardo was never afraid to think big. Most of his inventions were ahead of their time. Many were only produced centuries after his death.

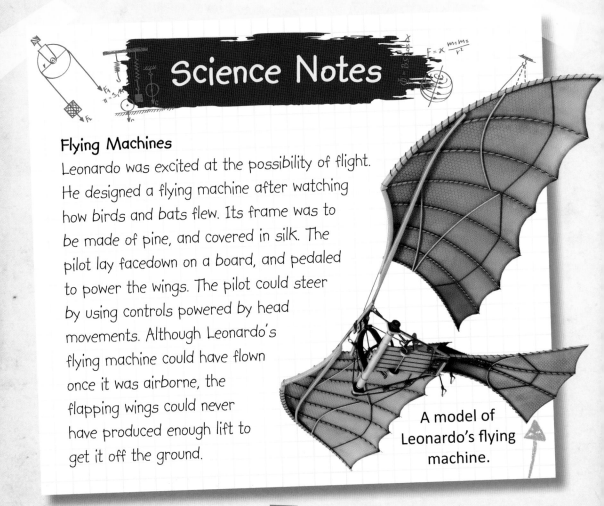

Science Notes

Flying Machines

Leonardo was excited at the possibility of flight. He designed a flying machine after watching how birds and bats flew. Its frame was to be made of pine, and covered in silk. The pilot lay facedown on a board, and pedaled to power the wings. The pilot could steer by using controls powered by head movements. Although Leonardo's flying machine could have flown once it was airborne, the flapping wings could never have produced enough lift to get it off the ground.

A model of Leonardo's flying machine.

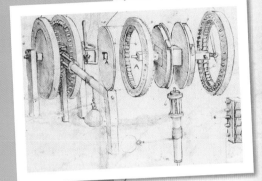
The first actual helicopter wasn't built until the 1940s, but Leonardo's sketch from the late 1400s showed a design of a similar flying machine. He never actually built and tested his design, known as an "aerial screw," but his notes and drawings showed exactly how it would work. Leonardo wrote: "If this instrument made with a screw be well made – that is to say, made of linen of which the pores are stopped up with starch and be turned swiftly, the said screw will make its spiral in the air and it will rise high."

His invention was similar to the way today's helicopters work. However, it was powered by four men standing on a platform, turning cranks, so modern scientists believe it would have been too heavy to lift into the air.

Leonardo's Final Years

Leonardo returned to Florence in 1503 and spent two years creating a **mural** for a room in the Old Palace. He drew an exciting battle scene from the Battle of Anghiari. Rival artist, Michelangelo, decorated the opposite wall with a painting of the Battle of Cascina.

Leonardo designed a clever platform that could be raised or folded like an accordion, to help him paint the tall mural. He also experimented using oil paint on a thick undercoat. Unfortunately the experiment didn't work, as the paint would not dry. Leonardo abandoned the project.

In the 1550s, another artist, Giorgio Vasari, was asked to paint over all the walls with new murals. Vasari admired Leonardo and would have been reluctant to paint over his work. In 2012, art historian Maurizio Seracini found evidence that Leonardo's painting still exists on a hidden inner wall underneath Vasari's mural! Seracini found a hidden wall, with evidence of paint on it. The paint was the same as paint used on Leonardo's *Mona Lisa*! Any more investigation would destroy Vasari's mural, though, which art historians do not want to do.

One of Leonardo's sketches for the lost *Battle of Anghiari* mural

Leonardo went back to Milan, where he was asked to make a mechanical lion for François I of France. The lion was designed to walk forward and open its chest to reveal a bunch of flowers!

Impressed, François asked Leonardo to work for him, and he was given a manor house, Clos Lucé, to live in. He spent the last three years of his life there, with his friend and apprentice, Francesco Melzi. Leonardo died at Clos Lucé on May 2, 1519. Vasari wrote that King François held Leonardo's head in his arms as he died.

A detail from a painting by Jean-Auguste-Dominique Ingres. François I holds the dying Leonardo da Vinci's head.

"As a well-spent day brings happy sleep, so a life well spent brings happy death."

LEONARDO DA VINCI

Science Project

Test Leonardo's Parachute

Another of Leonardo's inventions was the parachute. His drawing shows a sealed linen cloth held open by a pyramid of wooden poles. He noted next to his drawing that anyone could jump from any height without injury using his parachute. In 2000, skydiver Adrian Nicholas tested Leonardo's design, jumping out of a hot air balloon from 1.8 miles (3,000 m) up. The only modification made was to attach a harness to hold the parachutist in place. The parachute worked! Nicholas found the ride was smooth, but that the weight of the poles could injure a person when they landed.

You Will Need:

- A sheet of paper
- scissors
- glue stick
- two equal lengths of string
- paper clips

Copy this template onto your paper.

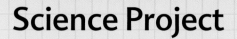

1

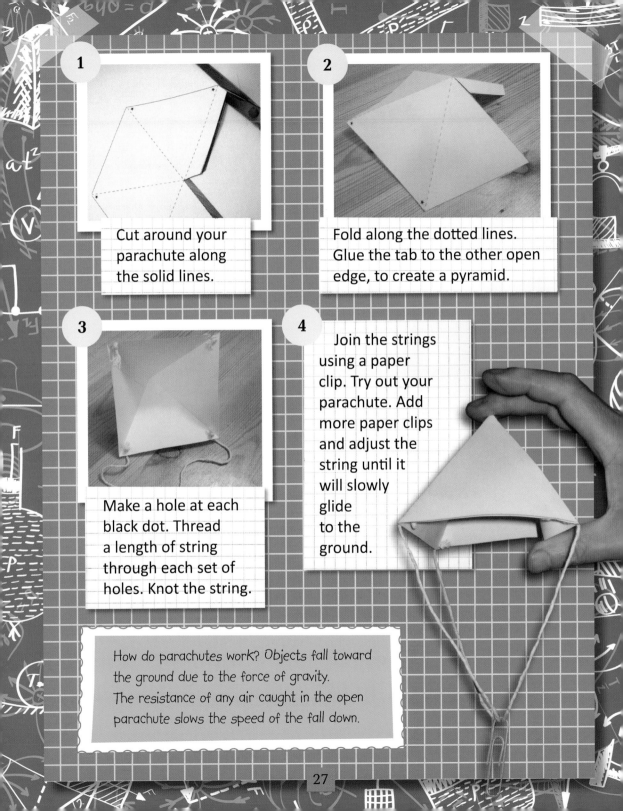

Cut around your parachute along the solid lines.

2

Fold along the dotted lines. Glue the tab to the other open edge, to create a pyramid.

3

Make a hole at each black dot. Thread a length of string through each set of holes. Knot the string.

4

Join the strings using a paper clip. Try out your parachute. Add more paper clips and adjust the string until it will slowly glide to the ground.

How do parachutes work? Objects fall toward the ground due to the force of gravity. The resistance of any air caught in the open parachute slows the speed of the fall down.

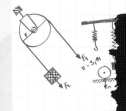

Test Your Knowledge

Test your science knowledge and your memory with this quiz about Leonardo da Vinci and his work. Can you get them all right? Answers are at the bottom of page 29.

1 Where was Leonardo da Vinci born?
a) Spain b) Canada c) Italy

2 What is Leonardo's most famous painting known as?
a) *The Haywain* b) *The Mona Lisa* c) *David*

3 What is anatomy?
a) the study of human or animal structure
b) a very small particle
c) a type of paint

4 Why should scientists keep a notebook?
a) to jot down their ideas
b) to keep a record of their experiments and their results
c) both a and b

5 What was "the Renaissance"?
a) a time of discovery b) a sculpture c) a painting

6 Why was Leonardo's giant horse statue never made?
a) it was too ugly
b) the metal needed was used for weapons instead
c) Leonardo never finished it

7 Which of these weapons did Leonardo invent?
a) armored tank   b) atomic bomb   c) boomerang

8 What was peculiar about many of Leonardo's written notes?
a) he wrote in Latin
b) he used green ink
c) he wrote backwards

9 What does a bird's-eye view map look like?
a) as if viewed from above
b) as if viewed from ground level

10 Why do engineers draw exploded diagrams?
a) to see each part clearly, and understand how they fit together
b) to show what would happen if a weapon exploded
c) they are not very good at drawing

Glossary

ammunition Objects such as bullets fired from guns.

anatomy The structural makeup especially of an organism or any of its parts.

apprentice A person learning a trade or art by experience under a skilled worker.

architect A person who designs buildings and advises in their construction.

casting Shaping a substance by pouring it in liquid or very soft form into a mold and letting it harden without pressure.

deflects Turns or causes to turn an object from its course.

exploded views A diagram of an object where the components are drawn slightly separated to show the relationship or order of assembly of various parts.

furnaces Enclosed structures in which heat is produced, used for heating a house or melting metals.

Latin The language of ancient Rome.

lyre A small harp held in the hands for playing.

molten Melted especially by very great heat.

mural A work of art applied to and made part of a wall surface.

parallel Lying or moving in the same direction but always the same distance apart.

politics The art of winning and holding control over a government.

reciprocating motion A repetitive up-and-down or back-and-forth linear motion.

Renaissance The period of European history between the 14th and 17th centuries marked by a flourishing of art and literature inspired by ancient times and by the beginnings of modern science.

Renaissance man A person with many talents or areas of knowledge.

social class A division of a society based on social and economic status.

survey To find out the size, shape, and position of an area of land.

For More Information

Democker, Michael. *Leonardo da Vinci* (Brush with Greatness). Kennett Square, PA: Purple Toad Pub Inc, 2016.

Harrison, Paul. *Leonardo da Vinci in 30 Seconds* (Kids 30 Second). London, UK: Ivy Kids, 2017.

Venezia, Mike. *Leonardo da Vinci* (Getting to Know the World's Greatest Artists). Danbury CT: Childrens Press, 2015.

Visconti, Guido. *The Genius of Leonardo da Vinci*. Bath, UK: Barefoot Books, 2016.

Websites
Due to the changing nature of Internet links, PowerKids Press has developed an online list of websites related to the subject of this book. This site is updated regularly. Please use this link to access the list:

www.powerkidslinks.com/wcs/davinci

Index